EASY GUITAR
WITH NOTES & TAB

BOB DYLAN

Cover photo Michael Ochs Archives/Stringer

ISBN 978-1-4803-6405-9

 Music Sales America

Exclusively Distributed By

HAL•LEONARD®
CORPORATION
7777 W. Bluemound Rd. P.O. Box 13819 Milwaukee, WI 53213

STRUM AND PICK PATTERNS

This chart contains the suggested strum and pick patterns that are referred to by number at the beginning of each song in this book. The symbols ⊓ and ∨ in the strum patterns refer to down and up strokes, respectively. The letters in the pick patterns indicate which right-hand fingers play which strings.

p = thumb
i = index finger
m = middle finger
a = ring finger

For example; Pick Pattern 2
is played: thumb - index - middle - ring

<table>
<tr><td>

Strum Patterns

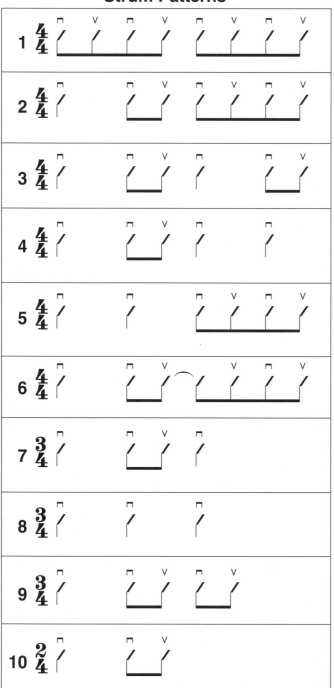

</td><td>

Pick Patterns

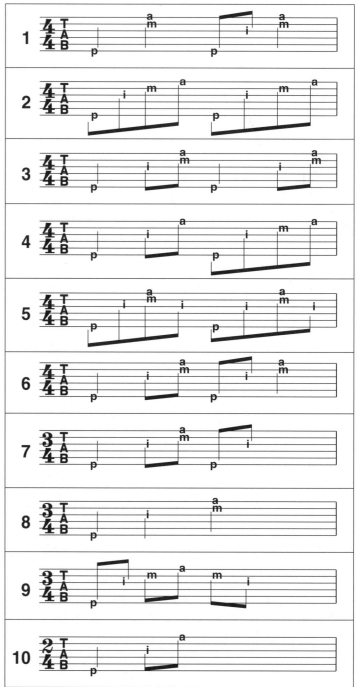

</td></tr>
</table>

You can use the 3/4 Strum and Pick Patterns in songs written in compound meter (6/8, 9/8, 12/8, etc.). For example, you can accompany a song in 6/8 by playing the 3/4 pattern twice in each measure. The 4/4 Strum and Pick Patterns can be used for songs written in cut time (¢) by doubling the note time values in the patterns. Each pattern would therefore last two measures in cut time.

CONTENTS

Blowin' in the Wind

Words and Music by Bob Dylan

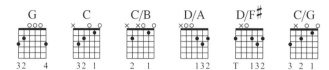

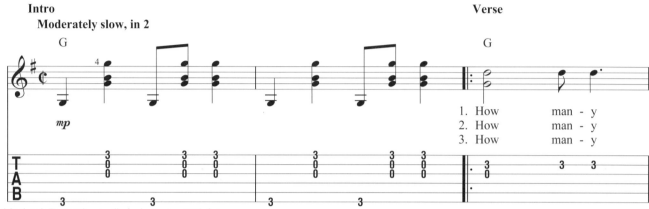

*Capo VII

Strum Pattern: 5
Pick Pattern: 1

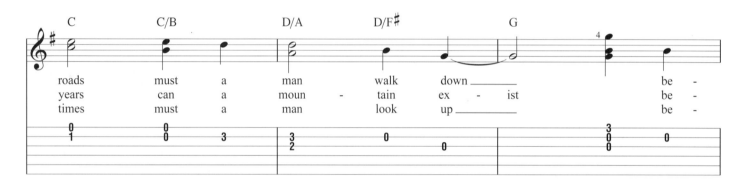

*Optional: To match recording, place capo at 7th fret.

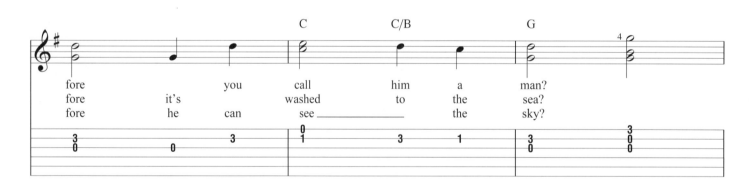

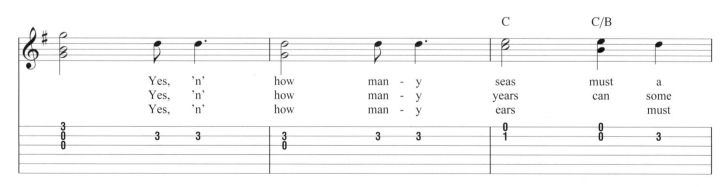

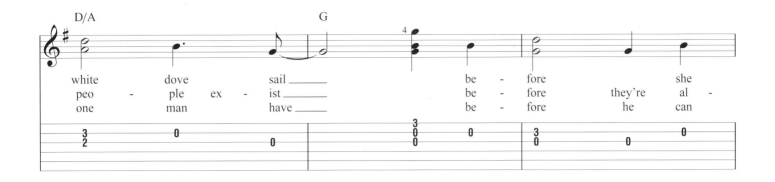

white dove sail _____ be - fore she
peo - ple ex - ist have _____ be - fore they're al -
one man before he can

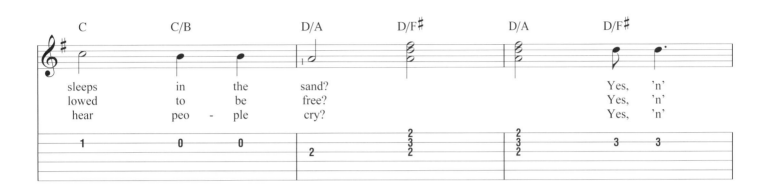

sleeps in the sand? Yes, 'n'
lowed to be free? Yes, 'n'
hear peo - ple cry? Yes, 'n'

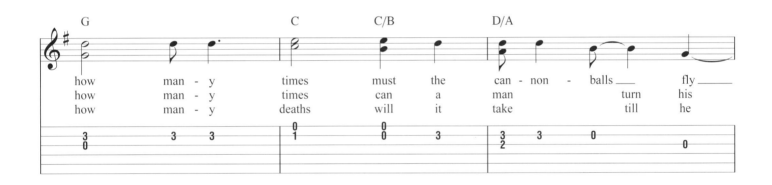

how man - y times must the can - non - balls _____ fly _____
how man - y times can a man turn his
how man - y deaths will it take till he

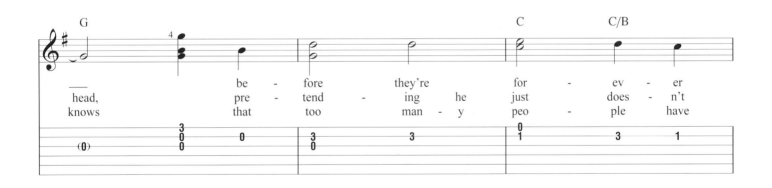

_____ be - fore they're for - ev - er
head, pre - tend - ing he just does - n't
knows that too man - y peo - ple have

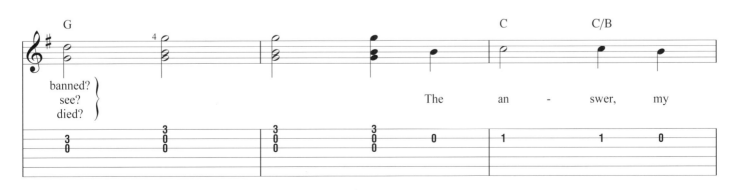

banned?
see? The an - swer, my
died?

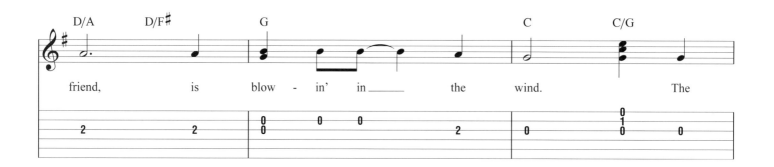

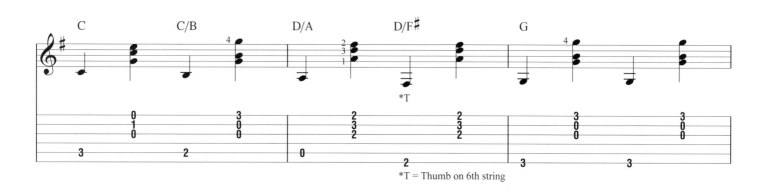

*T = Thumb on 6th string

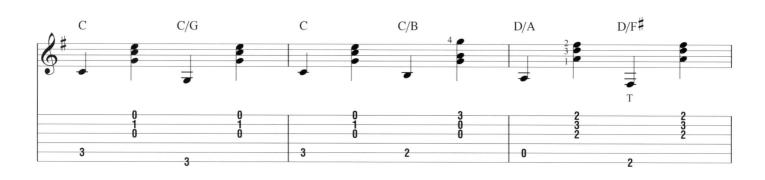

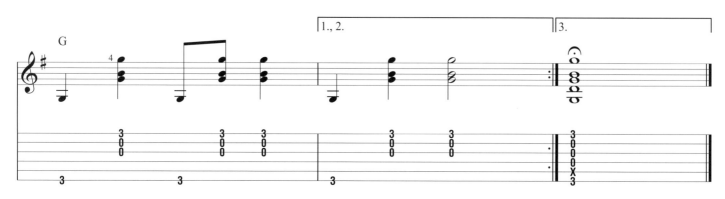

Don't Think Twice, It's All Right

Words and Music by Bob Dylan

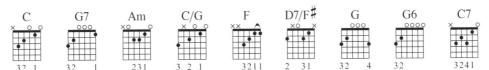

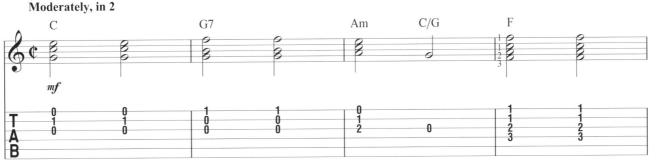

*Capo IV

Strum Pattern: 3
Pick Pattern: 1

Intro
Moderately, in 2

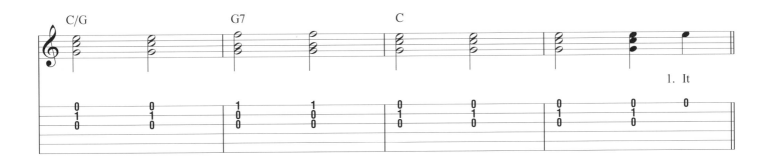

*Optional: To match recording, place capo at 4th fret.

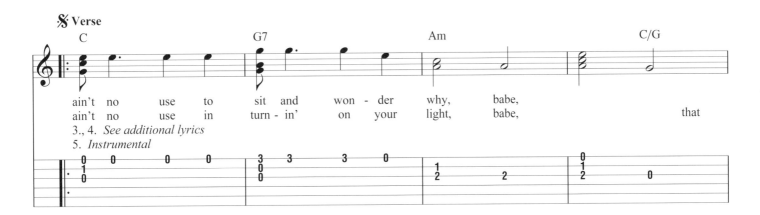

1. It

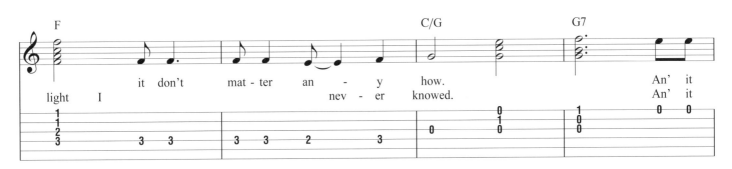

ain't no   use   to   sit and   won - der   why,   babe,   that
ain't no   use in   turn - in'   on your   light,   babe,
3., 4. *See additional lyrics*
5. *Instrumental*

light   I   it don't   mat - ter   an - y   how.
                      nev - er   knowed.
An' it
An' it

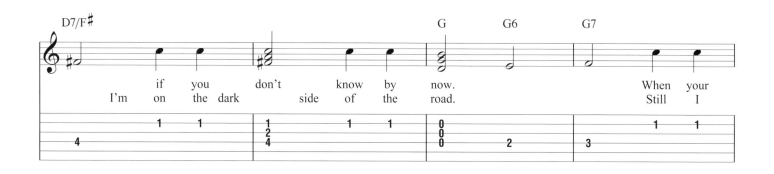

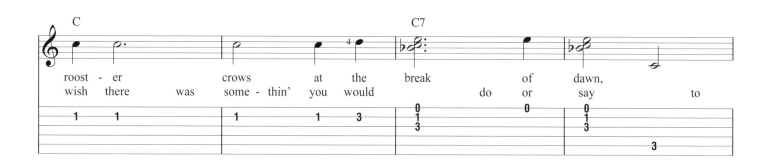

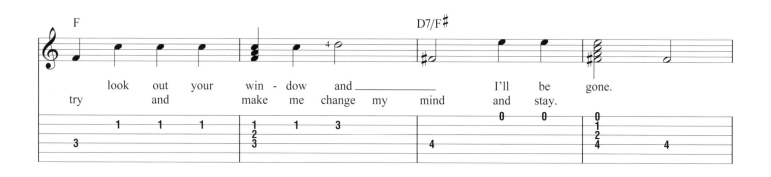

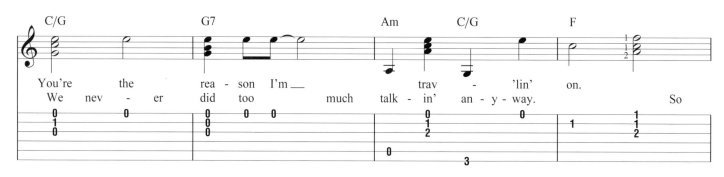

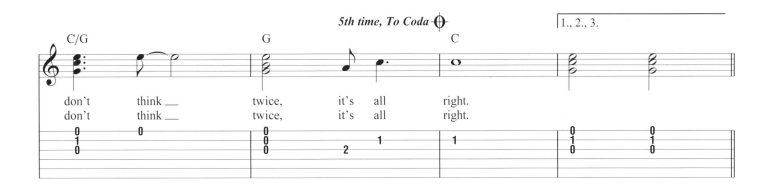

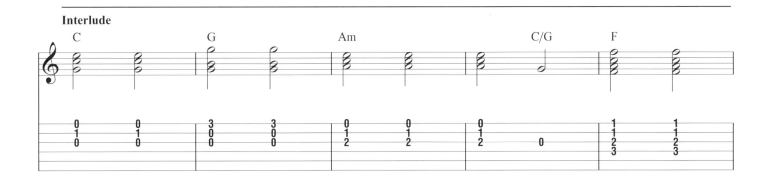

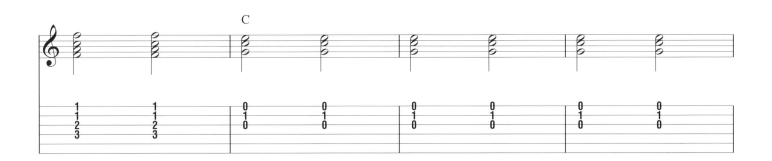

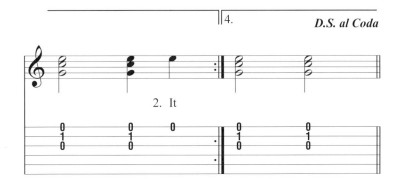

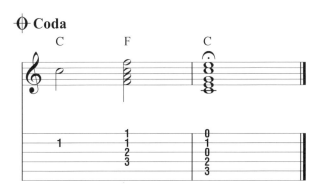

Additional Lyrics

3. It ain't no use in callin' out my name, gal,
   Like you never did before.
   It ain't no use in callin' out my name, gal,
   I can't hear you anymore.
   I'm a-thinkin' and a-wond'rin' all the way down the road
   I once loved a woman, a child I'm told.
   I give her my heart but she wanted my soul,
   But don't think twice, it's all right.

4. I'm walkin' down that long, lonesome road, babe,
   Where I'm bound, I can't tell.
   But goodbye's too good a word, gal,
   So I'll just say fare thee well.
   I ain't sayin' you treated me unkind,
   You could have done better but I don't mind.
   You just kinda wasted my precious time.
   But don't think twice, it's all right.

Hurricane

Words and Music by Bob Dylan and Jacques Levy

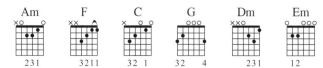

Strum Pattern: 1
Pick Pattern: 4

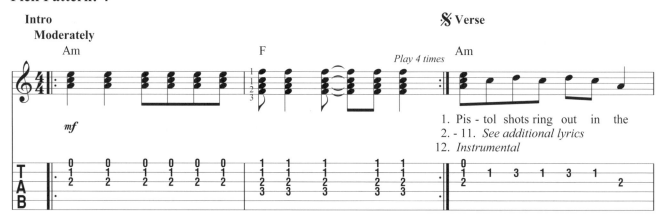

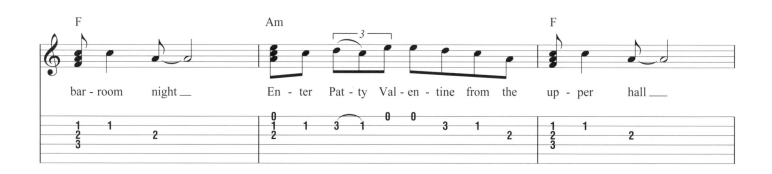

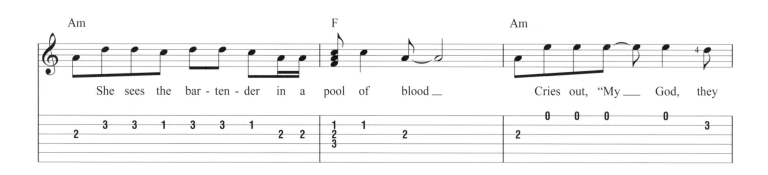

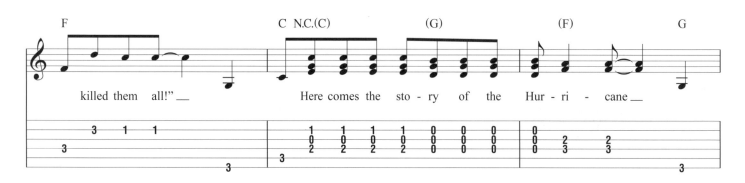

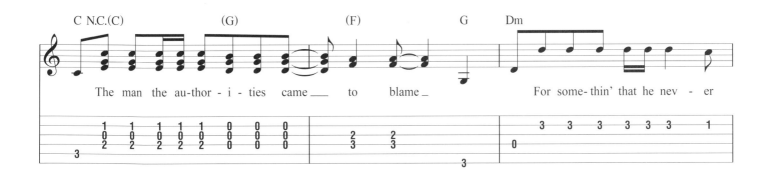

The man the au-thor-i-ties came ___ to blame ___ For some-thin' that he nev - er

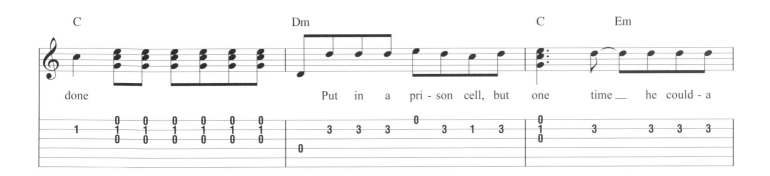

done Put in a pri-son cell, but one time ___ he could - a

To Coda ⊕ | 1. - 10. | **Interlude**

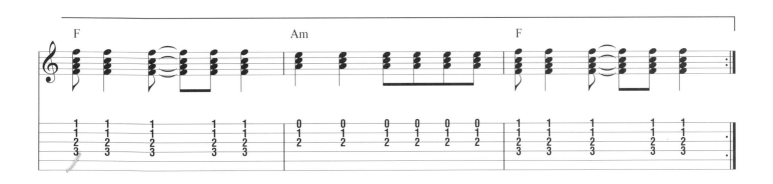

been the cham-pi-on of the world ___

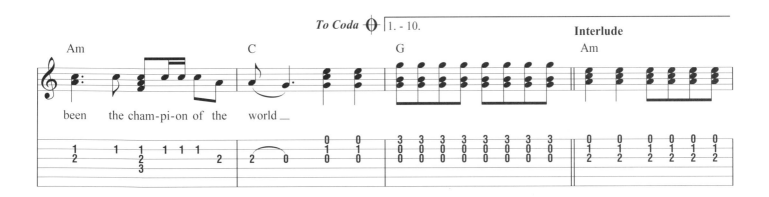

| 11. | **Interlude** | *4th time, D.S. al Coda* |

Play 4 times

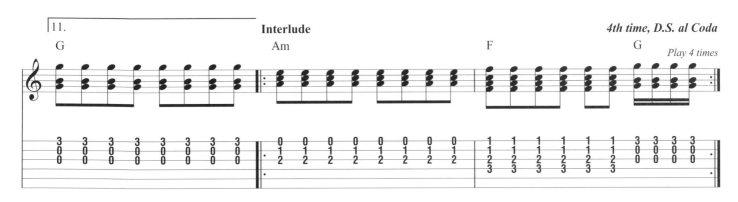

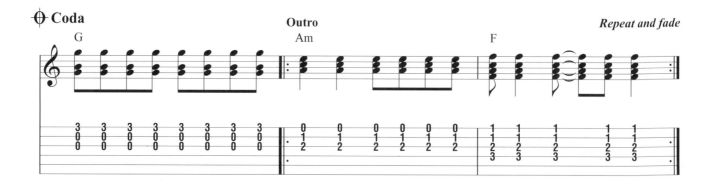

Additional Lyrics

2. Three bodies lyin' there does Patty see
   And another man named Bello, movin' around mysteriously
   "I didn't do it," he says, and he throws up his hands
   "I was only robbin' the register, I hope you understand
   I saw them leavin'," he says, and he stops
   "One of us had better call up the cops"
   And so Patty calls the cops
   And they arrive on the scene with their red lights flashin'
   In the hot New Jersey night

3. Meanwhile, far away in another part of town
   Rubin Carter and a couple of friends are drivin' around
   Number one contender for the middleweight crown
   Had no idea what kinda shit was about to go down
   When a cop pulled him over to the side of the road
   Just like the time before and time before that
   In Paterson that's just the way things go
   If you're black you might as well not show up on the street
   'Less you wanna draw the heat

4. Alfred Bello had a partner and he had a rap for the cops
   Him and Arthur Dexter Bradley were just out prowlin' around
   He said, "I saw two men runnin' out, they looked like middleweights
   They jumped into a white car with out-of-state plates"
   And Miss Patty Valentine just nodded her head
   Cop said, "Wait a minute, boys, this one's not dead"
   So they took him to the infirmary
   And though this man could hardly see
   They told him that he could identify the guilty men

5. Four in the mornin' and they haul Rubin in
   Take him to the hospital and they bring him upstairs
   The wounded man looks up through his one dyin' eye
   Says, "Wha'd you bring him in here for? He ain't the guy!"
   Yes, here's the story of the Hurricane
   The man the authorities came to blame
   For somethin' that he never done
   Put in a prison cell, but one time he could-a been
   The champion of the world

6. Four months later, the ghettos are in flame
   Rubin's in South America, fightin' for his name
   While Arthur Dexter Bradley's still in the robbery game
   And the cops are puttin' the screws to him, lookin' for somebody to blame
   "Remember that murder that you happened in a bar?"
   "Remember you said you saw the getaway car?"
   "You think you'd like to play ball with the law?"
   "Think it might-a been that fighter that you saw runnin' that night?"
   "Don't forget that you are white"

7. Arthur Dexter Bradley said, "I'm really not sure"
   Cops said, "A poor boy like you could use a break
   We got you for the motel job and we're talkin' to your friend Bello
   Now you don't wanta have to move back to jail, be a nice fellow
   You'll be doin' society a favor
   That sonofabitch is brave and gettin' braver
   We want to put his ass in stir
   We want to pin this triple murder on him
   He ain't no Gentleman Jim"

8. Rubin could take a man out with just one punch
   But he never did like to talk about it all that much
   It's my work, he'd say, and I do it for pay
   And when it's over I'd just as soon go on my way
   Up to some paradise
   Where the trout streams flow and the air is nice
   And ride a horse along a trail
   But then they took him to the jailhouse
   Where they try to turn a man into a mouse

9. All of Rubin's cards were marked in advance
   The trial was a pig-circus, he never had a chance
   The judge made Rubin's witnesses drunkards from the slums
   To the white folks who watched he was a revolutionary bum
   And to the black folks he was just a crazy nigger
   No one doubted that he pulled the trigger
   And though they could not produce the gun
   The D.A. said he was the one who did the deed
   And the all-white jury agreed

10. Rubin Carter was falsely tried
    The crime was murder "one," guess who testified?
    Bello and Bradley and they both baldly lied
    And the newspapers, they all went along for the ride
    How can the life of such a man
    Be in the palm of some fool's hand?
    To see him obviously framed
    Couldn't help but make me feel ashamed to live in a land
    Where justice is a game

11. Now all the criminals in their coats and their ties
    Are free to drink martinis and watch the sun rise
    While Rubin sits like Buddha in a ten-foot cell
    An innocent man in a living hell
    Yes, that's the story of the Hurricane
    But it won't be over till they clear his name
    And give him back the time he's done
    Put in a prison cell, but one time he could-a been
    The champion of the world

It Ain't Me Babe

Words and Music by Bob Dylan

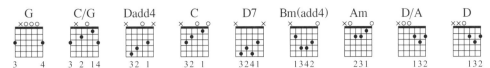

Strum Pattern: 3
Pick Pattern: 3

Intro
Moderately, in 2

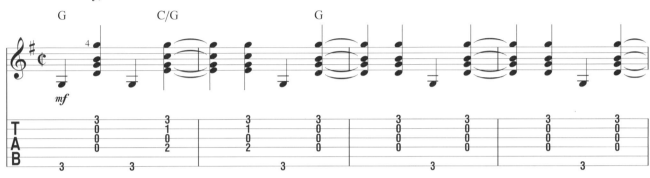

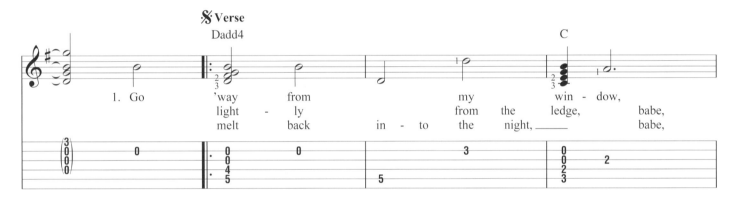

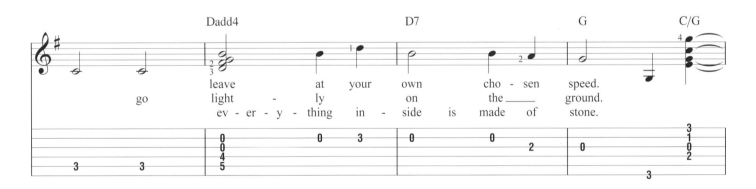

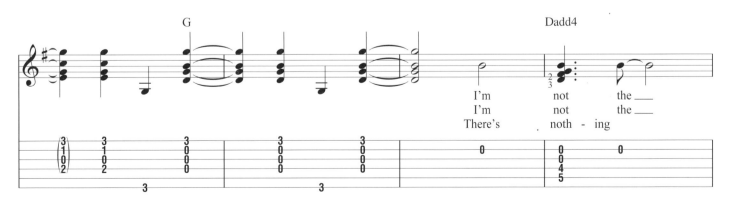

13

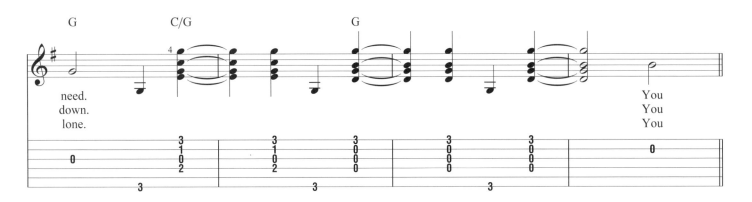

Pre-Chorus

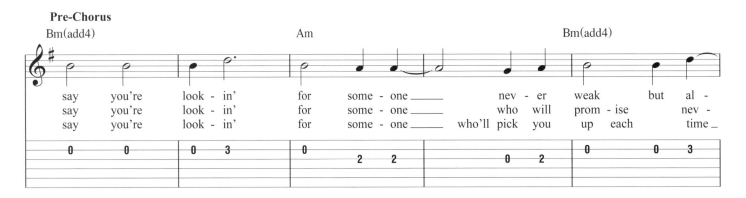

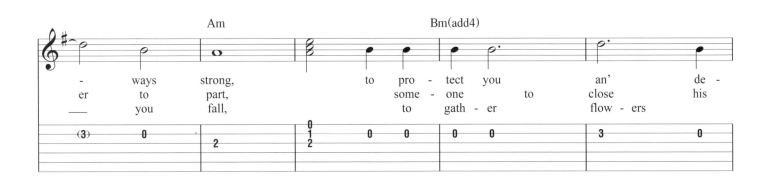

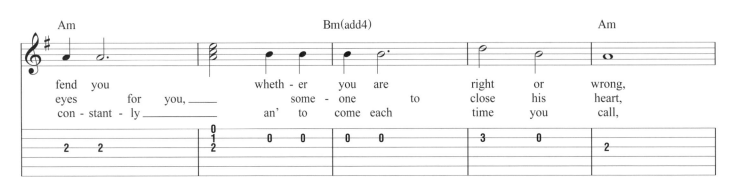

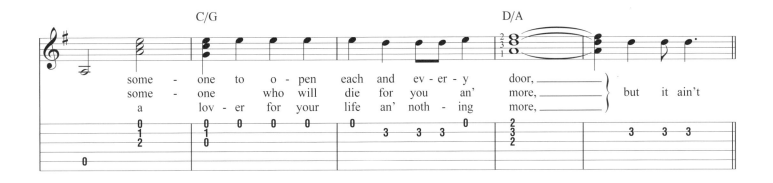

some - one to o - pen each and ev - er - y door, ___ but it ain't
some - one who will die for you an' more, ___
a lov - er for your life an' noth - ing more, ___

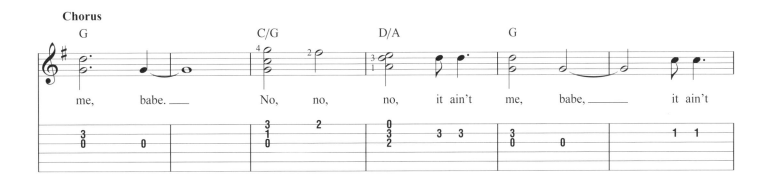

Chorus

me, babe. ___ No, no, no, it ain't me, babe, ___ it ain't

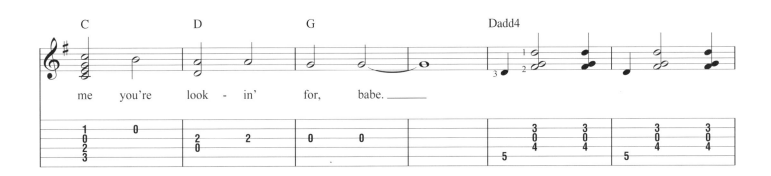

me you're look - in' for, babe. ___

3rd time, To Coda ⊕

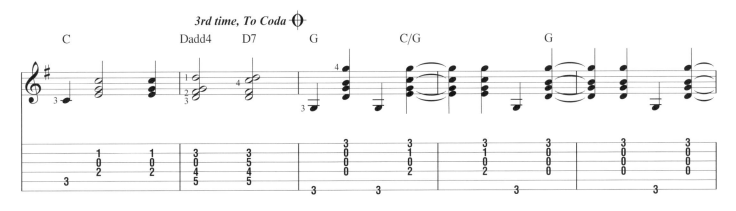

2nd time, D.S. al Coda

2. Go
3. Go

⊕ **Coda**

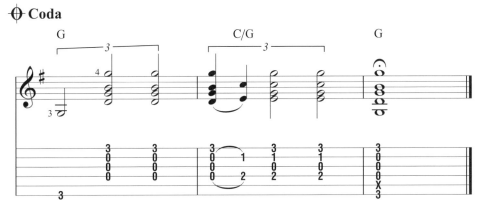

Knockin' on Heaven's Door

Words and Music by Bob Dylan

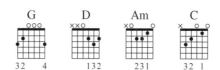

Strum Pattern: 3
Pick Pattern: 5

Intro
Moderately slow

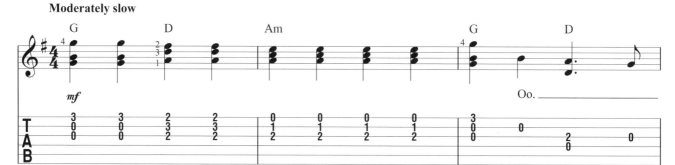

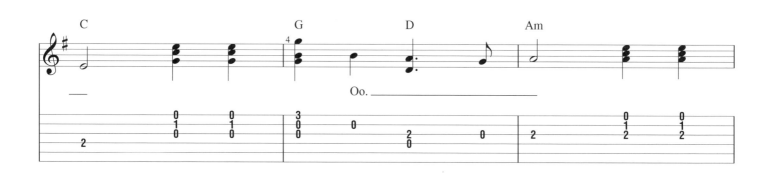

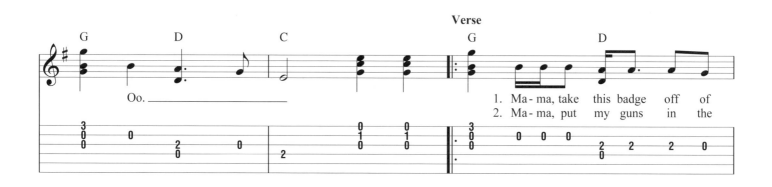

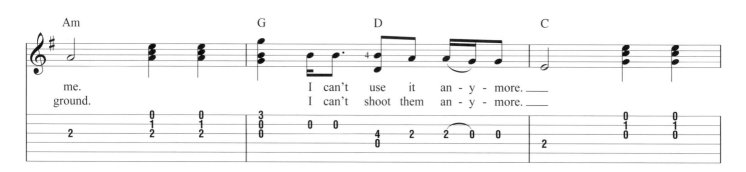

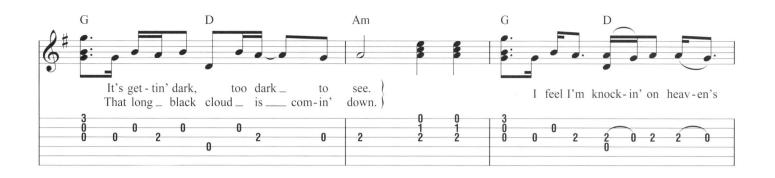

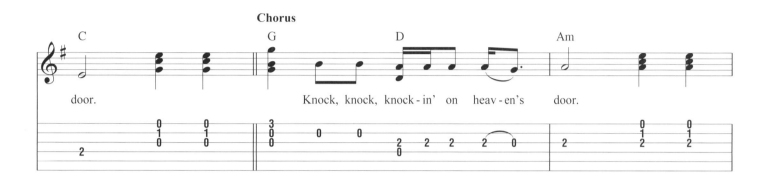

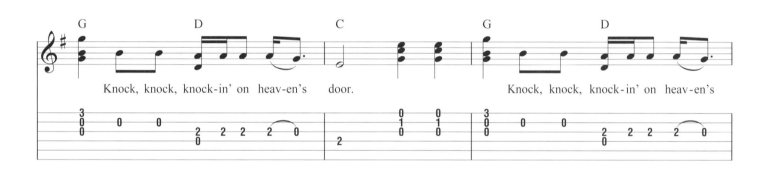

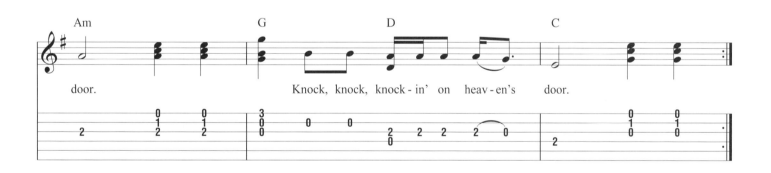

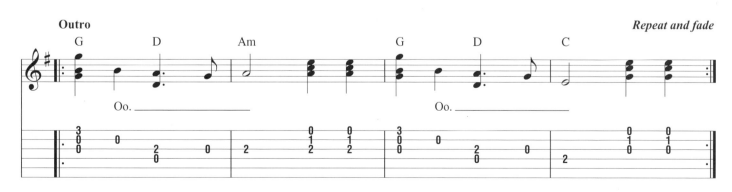

Lay Lady Lay

Words and Music by Bob Dylan

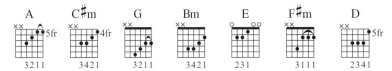

Strum Pattern: 1
Pick Pattern: 5

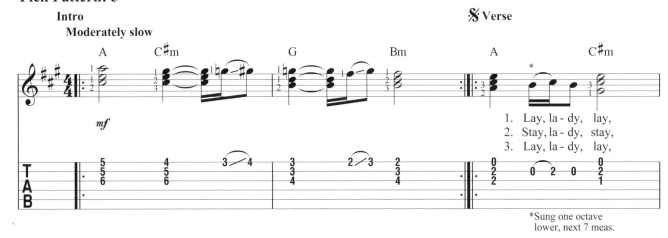

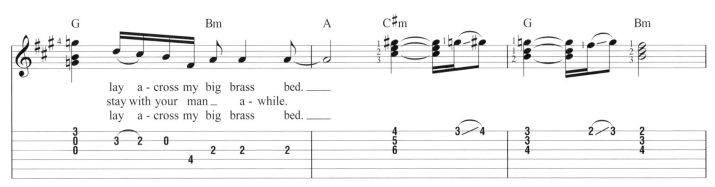

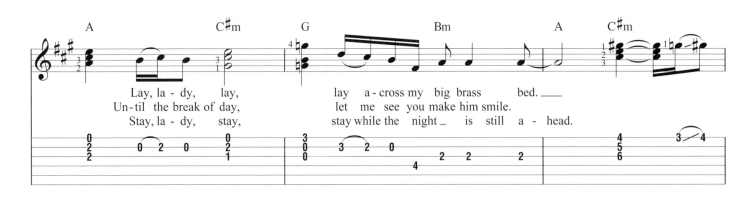

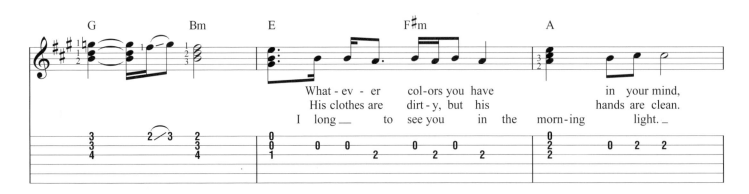

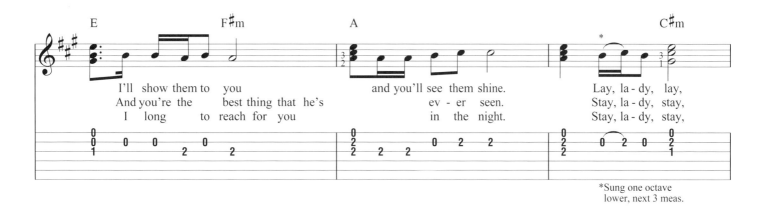

I'll show them to you   and you'll see them shine.
And you're the   best thing that he's   ev - er   seen.   Lay, la - dy, lay,
I   long   to reach for you   in   the night.   Stay, la - dy, stay,
     Stay, la - dy, stay,

*Sung one octave
lower, next 3 meas.

3rd time, To Coda ⊕

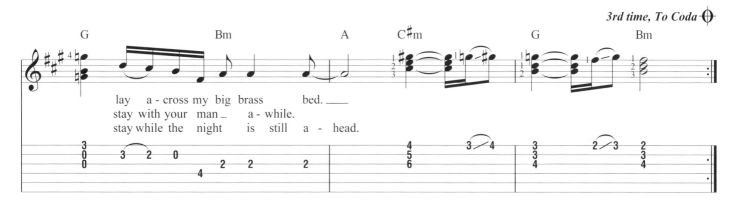

lay   a - cross my big brass   bed. ___
stay with your man _   a - while.
stay while the night   is still   a - head.

Bridge

Why wait an - y long - er   for the   world to   be - gin. ___   You can have your cake and eat   it   too. ___

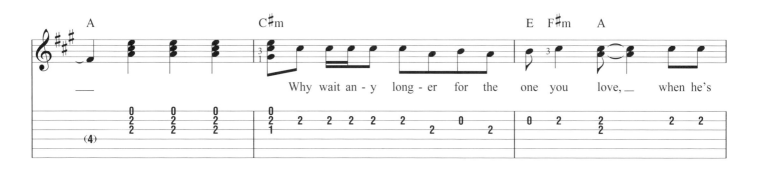

___   Why wait an - y   long - er   for the   one   you   love, ___   when he's

D.S. al Coda   ⊕ **Coda**

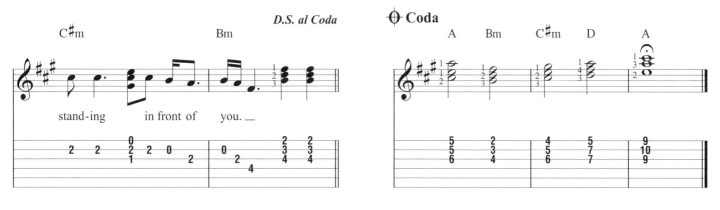

stand - ing   in front of   you. ___

Like a Rolling Stone

Words and Music by Bob Dylan

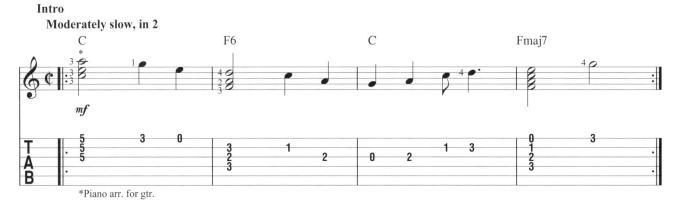

Strum Pattern: 3
Pick Pattern: 3

Intro
Moderately slow, in 2

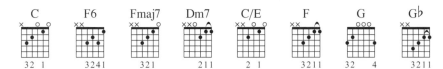

*Piano arr. for gtr.

% Verse

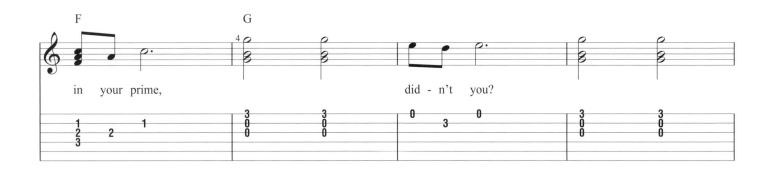

1. Once up - on _____ a time you dressed so fine, you threw the bums a dime
2., 3., 4. *See additional lyrics*

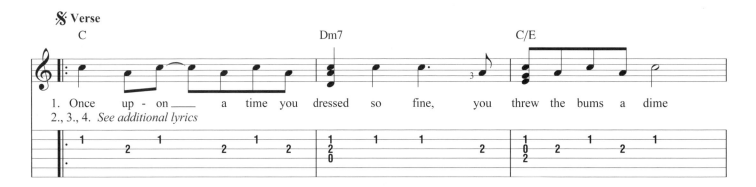

in your prime, did - n't you?

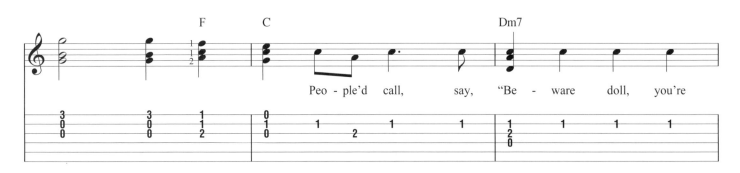

Peo - ple'd call, say, "Be - ware doll, you're

bound to fall." ___ You thought they were all

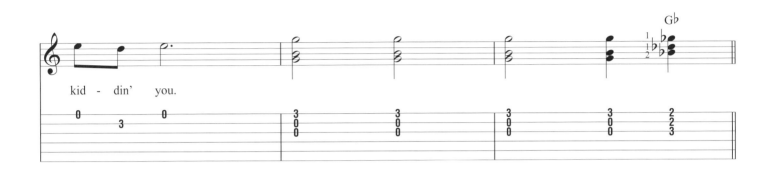

kid - din' you.

Pre-Chorus

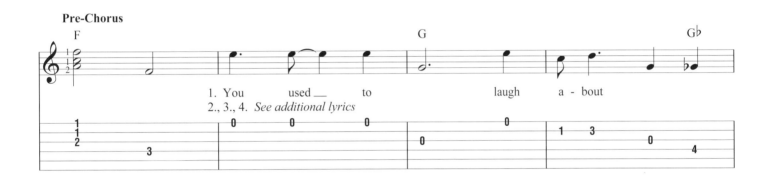

1. You used ___ to laugh a - bout
2., 3., 4. *See additional lyrics*

ev - 'ry - bod - y that was hang - in' out. ___

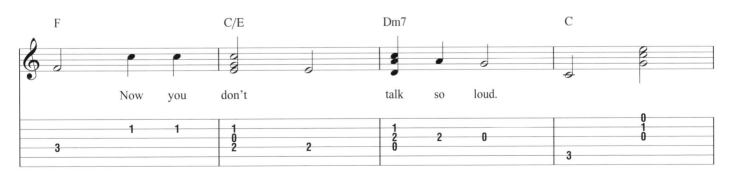

Now you don't talk so loud.

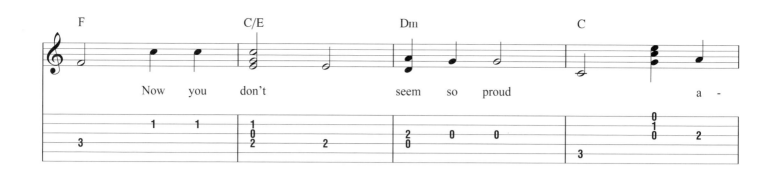

Now you don't   seem so proud   a -

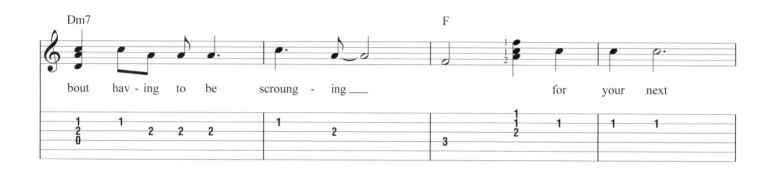

bout hav - ing to be scroung - ing _____   for your next

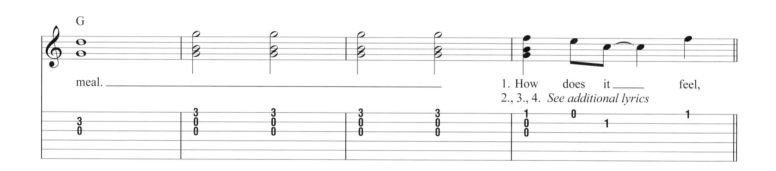

meal. _____   1. How does it _____ feel,
2., 3., 4. *See additional lyrics*

Chorus

how does it _____ feel

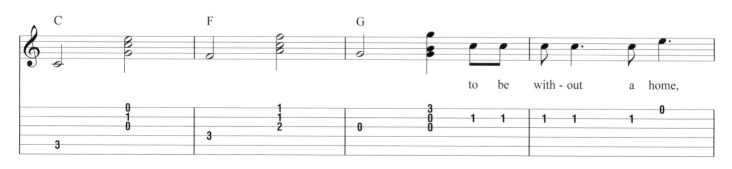

to be with - out a home,

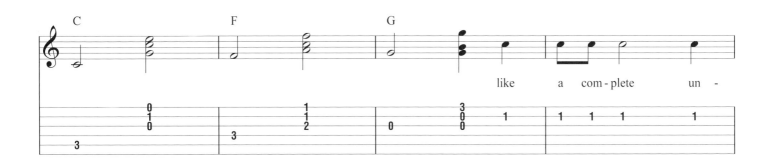

like   a   com -plete   un -

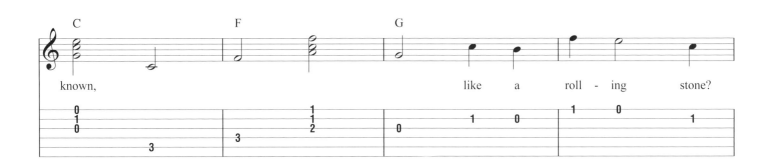

known,   like   a   roll - ing   stone?

4th time, To Coda ⊕

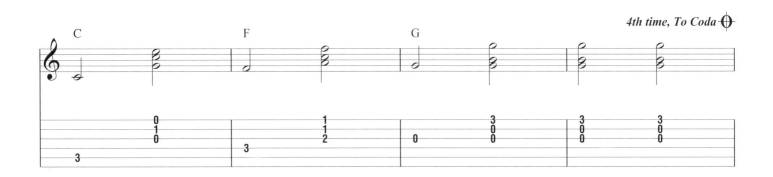

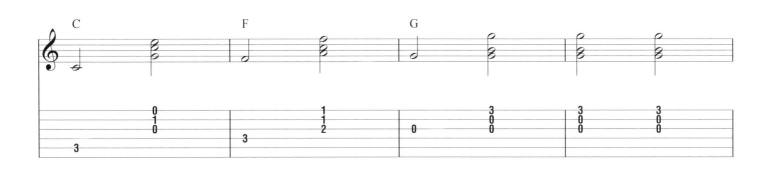

3rd time, D.S. al Coda

|1., 2.   ‖3.

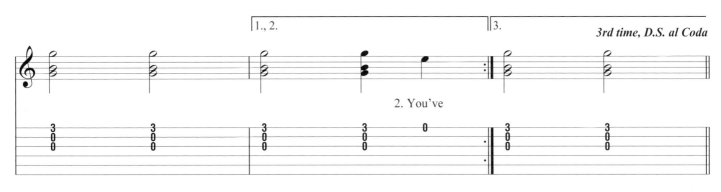

2. You've

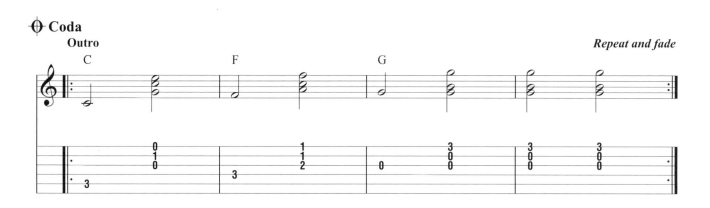

Additional Lyrics

2. You've gone to the finest school all right, Miss Lonely,
   But you know you only used to get juiced in it.
   And nobody has ever taught you how to live on the street
   And now you find out you're gonna have to get used to it.

Pre-Chorus 2 You said you'd never compromise
   With the mystery tramp, but now you realize
   He's not selling any alibis
   As you stare into the vacuum of his eyes
   And ask him do you want to make a deal?

Chorus 2 How does it feel,
   How does it feel
   To be on your own
   With no direction home
   Like a complete unknown,
   Like a rolling stone?

3. You never turned around to see the frowns on the jugglers and the clowns
   When they all come down and did tricks for you.
   You never understood that it ain't no good.
   You shouldn't let other people get your kicks for you

Pre-Chorus 3 You used to ride on the chrome horse with your diplomat
   Who carried on his shoulder a Siamese cat.
   Ain't it hard when you discover that
   He really wasn't where it's at
   After he took from you everything he could steal.

Chorus 3 Repeat Chorus 2

4. Princess on the steeple and all the pretty people,
   They're drinkin', thinkin' that they got it made,
   Exchanging all kinds of precious gifts and things.
   But you'd better lift your diamond ring, you'd better pawn it babe.

Pre-Chorus 4 You used to be so amused
   At Napoleon in rags and the language that he used.
   Go to him now, he calls you, you can't refuse.
   When you got nothing, you got nothing to lose.
   You're invisible now, you got no secrets to conceal.

Chorus 4 Repeat Chorus 2

Mr. Tambourine Man

Words and Music by Bob Dylan

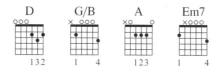

*Drop D tuning, capo III:

Strum Pattern: 1, 3
Pick Pattern: 3, 5

Intro
Moderately, in 2

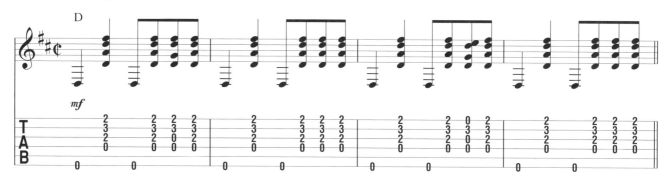

*Optional: To match recording, place capo at 3rd fret.

Chorus

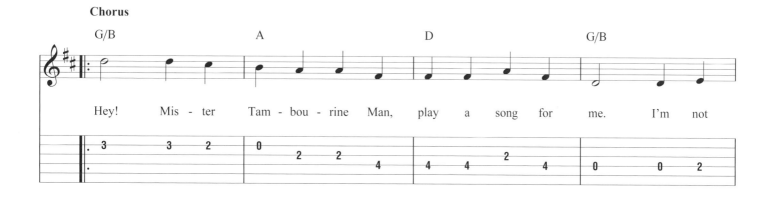

Hey! Mis - ter Tam - bou - rine Man, play a song for me. I'm not

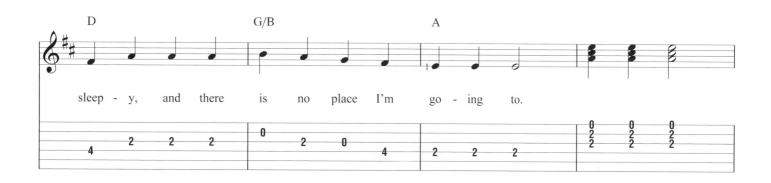

sleep - y, and there is no place I'm go - ing to.

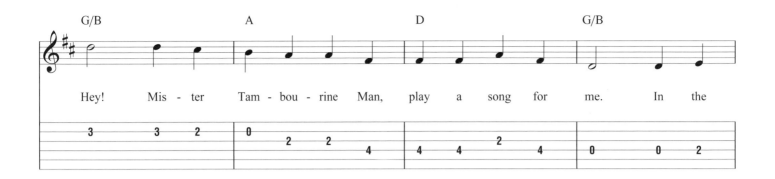

Hey! Mis - ter Tam - bou - rine Man, play a song for me. In the

To Coda ⊕

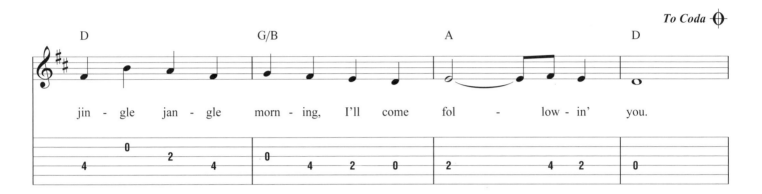

jin - gle jan - gle morn - ing, I'll come fol - low - in' you.

%**Verse**

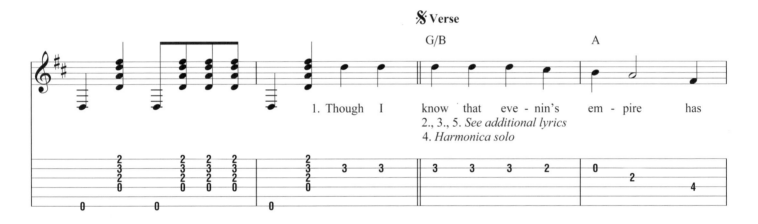

1. Though I know that eve - nin's em - pire has
2., 3., 5. *See additional lyrics*
4. *Harmonica solo*

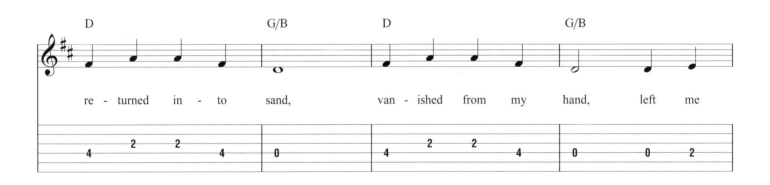

re - turned in - to sand, van - ished from my hand, left me

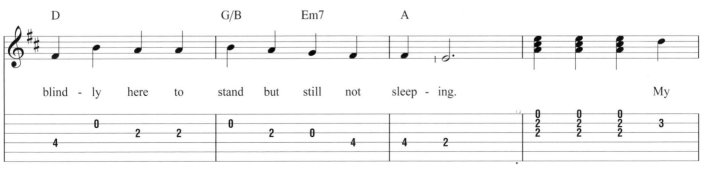

blind - ly here to stand but still not sleep - ing. My

wear - i - ess a - maz - es me, I'm brand - ed on my feet, I

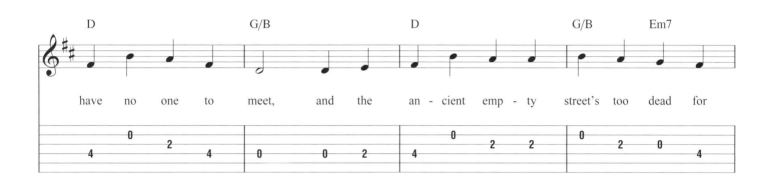

have no one to meet, and the an - cient emp - ty street's too dead for

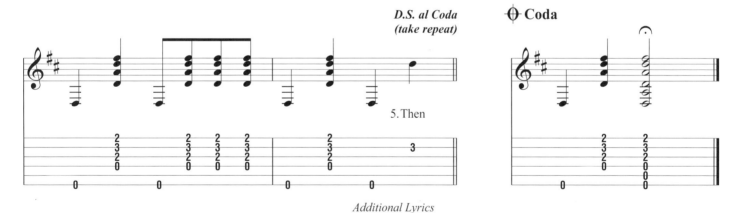

dream - ing.

D.S. al Coda
(take repeat)

⊕ **Coda**

5. Then

Additional Lyrics

2. Take me on a trip upon your magic swirlin' ship,
   My senses have been stripped, my hands can't feel to grip.
   My toes too numb to step, wait only for my boot heels
   To be wanderin'.
   I'm ready to go anywhere, I'm ready for to fade
   Into my own parade, cast your dancing spell my way,
   I promise to go under it.

3. Though you might hear laughin', spinnin', swingin' madly across the sun,
   It's not aimed at anyone, it's just escapin' on the run,
   And but for the sky there are no fences facin',
   And if you hear vague traces of skippin' reels of rhyme,
   To your tambourine in time, it's just a ragged clown behind,
   I wouldn't pay it any mind, it's just a shadow you're
   Seein' that he's chasing.

5. Then take me disappearin' through the smoke rings of my mind,
   Down the foggy ruins of time, far past the frozen leaves,
   The haunted, frightened trees out to the windy beach,
   Far from the twisted reach of crazy sorrow.
   Yes, to dance beneath the diamond sky with one hand waving free,
   Silhouetted by the sea, circled by the circus sands,
   With all memory and fate driven deep beneath the waves.
   Let me forget about today until tomorrow.

Positively 4th Street

Words and Music by Bob Dylan

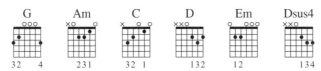

*Tune down 1/2 step:
(low to high) Eb-Ab-Db-Gb-Bb-Eb

Strum Pattern: 5
Pick Pattern: 1

Intro
Moderately

*Optional: To match recording, tune down 1/2 step.

Verse

1. You got a _____ lot-ta nerve to
2. - 6. *See additional lyrics*
7. *Instrumental*

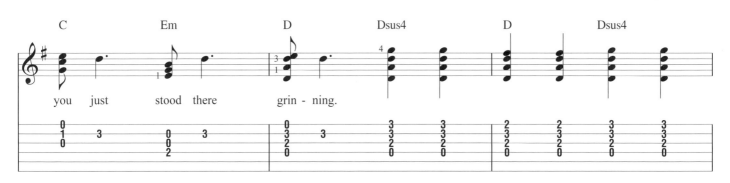

say you are _____ my _____ friend. When I was down

you just stood there grin-ning.

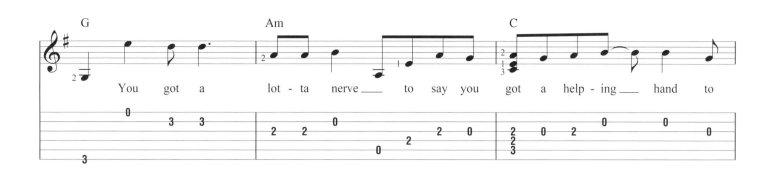

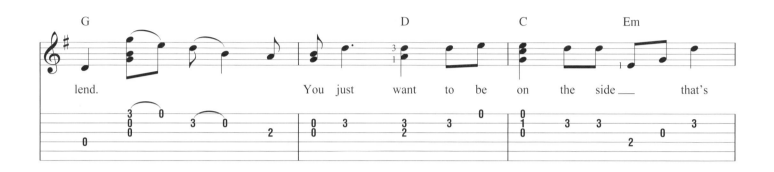

Play 7 times and fade

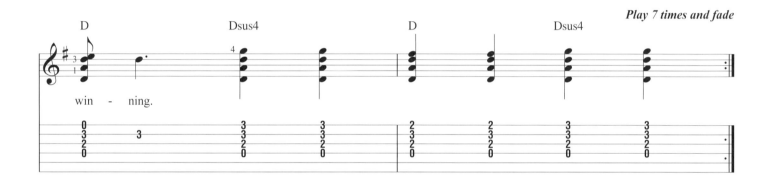

Additional Lyrics

2. You say I let you down,
   You know it's not like that.
   If you're hurt, why, then, don't you show it?
   You say you lost your faith,
   But that's not where it's at.
   You had no faith to lose, and you know it.

3. I know the reason
   That you talk behind my back.
   I used to be among the crowd you're in with.
   Do you take me for such a fool
   To think that I'd make contact
   With the one who tries to hide what he don't know to begin with?

4. You see me on the street,
   You always act surprised.
   You say, "How are you? Good luck,"
   But you don't mean it,
   When you know as well as me
   You'd rather see me paralyzed.
   Why don't you just come out once and scream it?

5. No, I do not feel that good
   When I see the heartbreaks you embrace.
   If I was a master thief, perhaps I'd rob them.
   And now I know you're dissatisfied
   With your position and your place.
   Don't you understand, it's not my problem.

6. I wish that for just one time
   You could stand inside my shoes,
   And just for that one moment I could be you.
   Yes, I wish that for just one time
   You could stand inside my shoes.
   You'd know what a drag it is to see you.

Shelter from the Storm

Words and Music by Bob Dylan

Strum Pattern: 5
Pick Pattern: 1

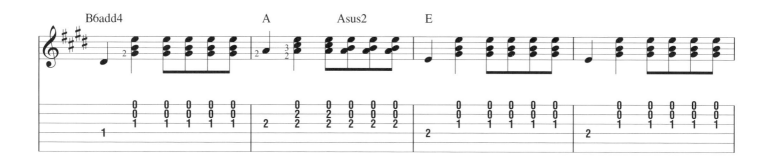

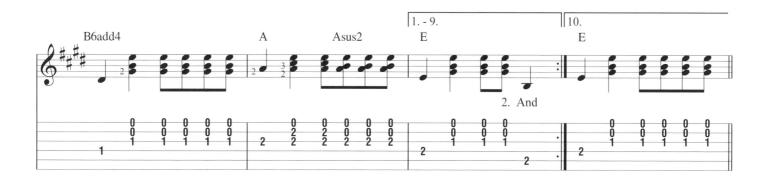

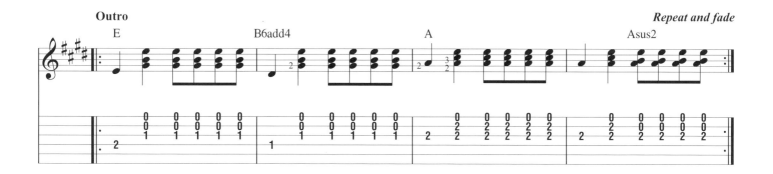

Additional Lyrics

2. And if I pass this way again, you can rest assured
   I'll always do my best for her, on that I give my word.
   In a world of steel-eyed death, and men who are fighting to be warm,
   "Come in," she said, "I'll give you shelter from the storm."

3. Not a word was spoke between us, there was little risk involved.
   Everything up to that point had been left unresolved.
   Try imagining a place where it's always safe and warm.
   "Come in," she said, "I'll give you shelter from the storm."

4. I was burned out from exhaustion, buried in the hail.
   Poisoned in the bushes an' blown out on the trail.
   Hunted like a crocodile, ravaged in the corn.
   "Come in," she said, "I'll give you shelter from the storm."

5. Suddenly I turned around and she was standin' there
   With silver bracelets on her wrists and flowers in her hair.
   She walked up to me so gracefully and took my crown of thorns.
   "Come in," she said, "I'll give you shelter from the storm."

6. Now there's a wall between us, somethin' there's been lost.
   I took too much for granted, got my signals crossed.
   Just to think it all began on a long-forgotten morn.
   "Come in," she said, "I'll give you shelter from the storm."

7. Well, the deputy walks on hard nails and the preacher rides a mount.
   But nothing really matters much, it's doom alone that counts.
   And the one-eyed undertaker, he blows a futile horn.
   "Come in," she said, "I'll give you shelter from the storm."

8. I've heard newborn babies wailin' like a mournin' dove
   And old men with broken teeth stranded without love.
   Do I understand your question, man, is it hopeless and forlorn?
   "Come in," she said, "I'll give you shelter from the storm."

9. In a little hilltop village, they gambled for my clothes.
   I bargained for salvation an' she gave me a lethal dose.
   I offered up my innocence and got repaid with scorn.
   "Come in," she said, "I'll give you shelter from the storm."

10. Well, I'm livin' in a foreign country but I'm bound to cross the line.
    Beauty walks a razor's edge, someday I'll make it mine.
    If I could only turn back the clock to when God and her were born.
    "Come in," she said, "I'll give you shelter from the storm."

The Times They Are A-Changin'

Words and Music by Bob Dylan

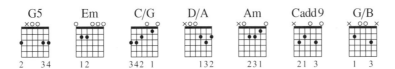

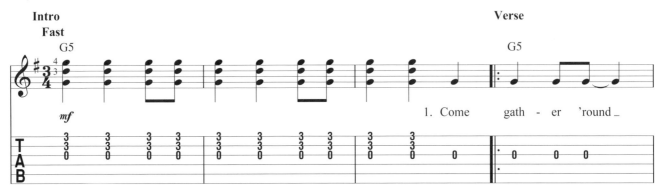

Strum Pattern: 7
Pick Pattern: 7

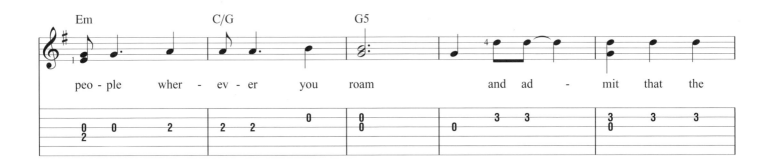

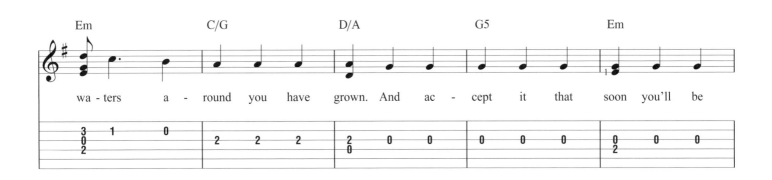

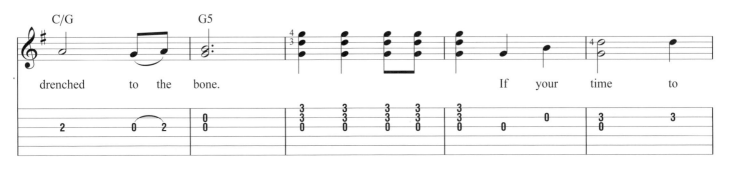

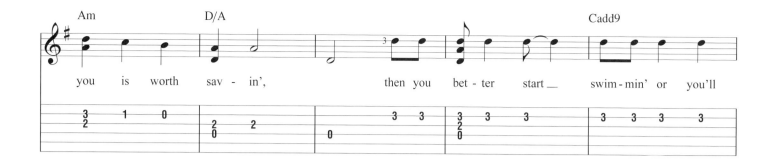

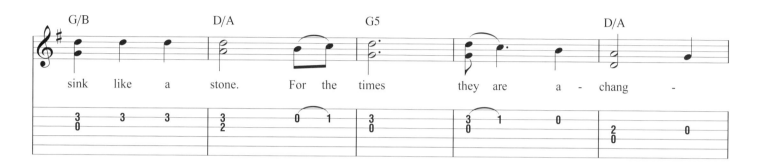

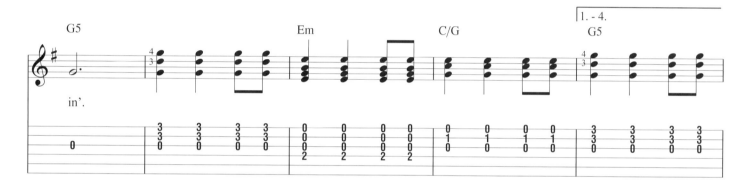

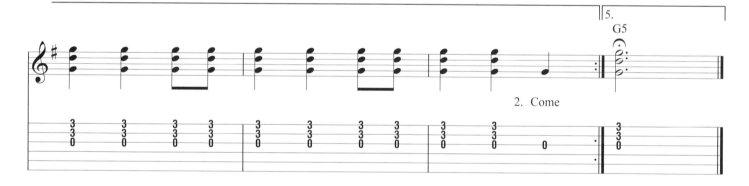

Additional Lyrics

2. Come writers and critics who prophesize with your pen
   And keep your eyes wide the chance won't come again.
   And don't speak too soon for the wheel's still in spin,
   And there's no tellin' who that it's namin'.
   For the loser now will be later to win.
   For the times they are a-changin'.

3. Come senators, congressmen please heed the call.
   Don't stand in the doorway, don't block up the hall.
   For he that gets hurt will be he who has stalled.
   There's a battle outside and it is ragin'.
   It'll soon shake your windows and rattle your walls
   For the times they are a-changin'.

4. Come mothers and fathers throughout the land,
   And don't criticize what you can't understand.
   Your sons and your daughters are beyond your command.
   Your old road is rapidly agin'.
   Please get out of the new one if you can't lend your hand.
   For the times they are a-changin'.

5. The line it is drawn, the curse it is cast,
   The slow one now will later be fast.
   As the present now will later be past.
   The order is rapidly fadin'.
   And the first one now will later be last,
   For the times they are a-changin'.

Tangled Up in Blue

Words and Music by Bob Dylan

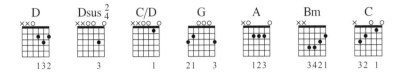

Strum Pattern: 2, 3
Pick Pattern: 2, 4

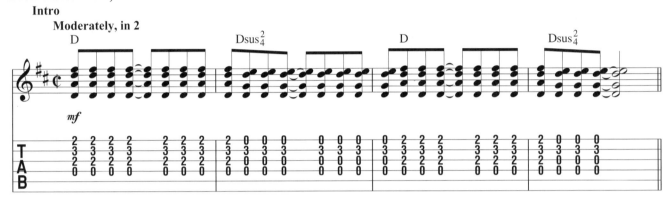

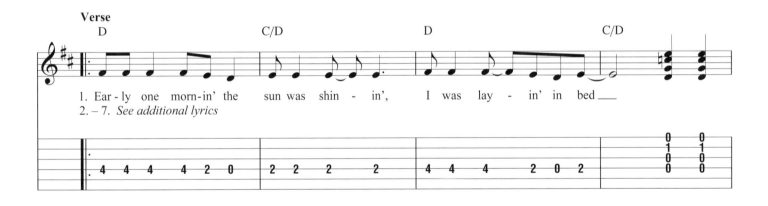

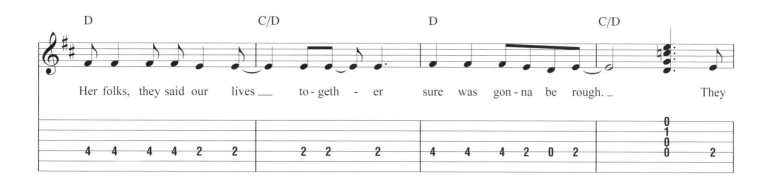

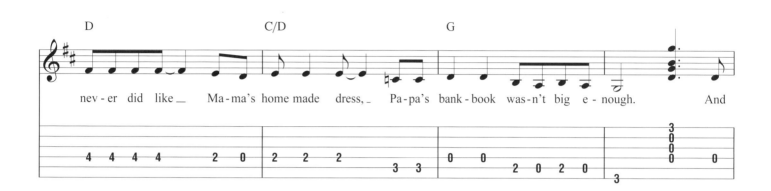

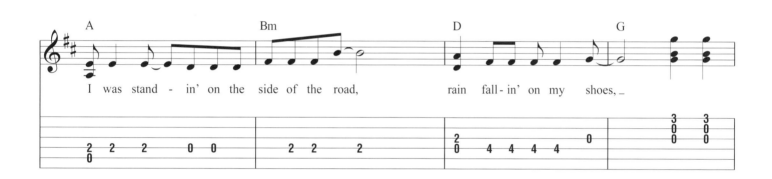

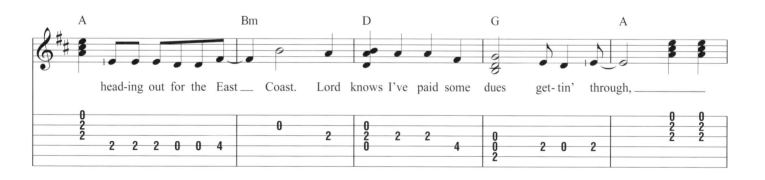

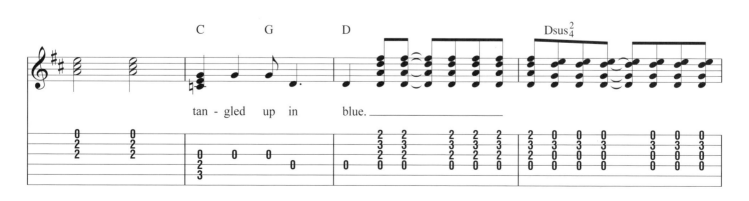

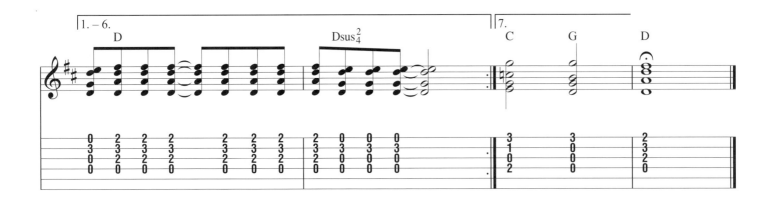

Additional Lyrics

2. She was married when we first met
   Soon to be divorced.
   I helped her out of a jam, I guess
   But I used a little too much force.
   We drove that car as far as we could,
   Abandoned it out West.
   Split up on a dark sad night,
   Both agreeing it was best.
   She turned around to look at me
   As I was walkin' away,
   I heard her say over my shoulder,
   "We'll meet again some day
   On the avenue,"
   Tangled up in blue.

3. I had a job in the great north woods
   Working as a cook for a spell,
   But I never did like it all that much,
   And one day the ax just fell.
   So I drifted down to New Orleans
   Where I happened to be employed
   Workin' for a while on a fishin' boat
   Right outside of Delacroix.
   But all the while I was alone
   The past was close behind,
   I seen a lot of women
   But she never escaped my mind,
   And I just grew,
   Tangled up in blue.

4. She was workin' in a topless place
   And I stopped in for a beer.
   I just kept lookin' at the side of her face
   In the spotlight so clear.
   And later on as the crowd thinned out,
   I's just about to do the same,
   She was standing there in back of my chair,
   Said to me, "Don't I know your name?"
   I muttered somethin' underneath my breath,
   She studied the lines on my face.
   I must admit I felt a little uneasy
   When she bent down to tie the laces
   Of my shoe,
   Tangled up in blue.

5. She lit a burner on the stove
   And offered me a pipe,
   "I thought you'd never say hello," she said,
   "You look like the silent type."
   Then she opened up a book of poems
   And handed it to me,
   Written by an Italian poet
   From the thirteenth century.
   And every one of them words rang true
   And glowed like burnin' coal
   Pourin' off of every page
   Like it was written in my soul
   From me to you,
   Tangled up in blue.

6. I lived with them on Montague Street
   In a basement down the stairs,
   There was music in the cafés at night
   And revolution in the air.
   Then he started into dealing with slaves
   And something inside of him died,
   She had to sell everything she owned
   And froze up inside.
   And when finally the bottom fell out
   I became withdrawn.
   The only thing I knew how to do
   Was to keep on keepin' on
   Like a bird that flew,
   Tangled up in blue.

7. So now I'm goin' back again,
   I got to get her somehow,
   All the people we used to know,
   They're an illusion to me now.
   Some are mathematicians,
   Some are carpenters' wives.
   Don't know how it all got started,
   I don't know what they're doin' with their lives.
   But me, I'm still on the road
   Headin' for another joint,
   We always did feel the same,
   We just saw it from a different point
   Of view,
   Tangled up in blue.

EASY GUITAR WITH NOTES & TAB

This series features simplified arrangements with notes, tab, chord charts, and strum and pick patterns.

MIXED FOLIOS

00702287	Acoustic	$19.99
00702002	Acoustic Rock Hits for Easy Guitar	$15.99
00702166	All-Time Best Guitar Collection	$19.99
00702232	Best Acoustic Songs for Easy Guitar	$16.99
00119835	Best Children's Songs	$16.99
00703055	The Big Book of Nursery Rhymes & Children's Songs	$16.99
00698978	Big Christmas Collection	$19.99
00702394	Bluegrass Songs for Easy Guitar	$15.99
00289632	Bohemian Rhapsody	$19.99
00703387	Celtic Classics	$14.99
00224808	Chart Hits of 2016-2017	$14.99
00267383	Chart Hits of 2017-2018	$14.99
00334293	Chart Hits of 2019-2020	$16.99
00702149	Children's Christian Songbook	$9.99
00702028	Christmas Classics	$8.99
00101779	Christmas Guitar	$14.99
00702141	Classic Rock	$8.95
00159642	Classical Melodies	$12.99
00253933	Disney/Pixar's Coco	$16.99
00702203	CMT's 100 Greatest Country Songs	$34.99
00702283	The Contemporary Christian Collection	$16.99
00196954	Contemporary Disney	$19.99
00702239	Country Classics for Easy Guitar	$24.99

00702257	Easy Acoustic Guitar Songs	$16.99
00702041	Favorite Hymns for Easy Guitar	$12.99
00222701	Folk Pop Songs	$17.99
00126894	Frozen	$14.99
00333922	Frozen 2	$14.99
00702286	Glee	$16.99
00702160	The Great American Country Songbook	$19.99
00702148	Great American Gospel for Guitar	$14.99
00702050	Great Classical Themes for Easy Guitar	$9.99
00275088	The Greatest Showman	$17.99
00148030	Halloween Guitar Songs	$14.99
00702273	Irish Songs	$12.99
00192503	Jazz Classics for Easy Guitar	$16.99
00702275	Jazz Favorites for Easy Guitar	$17.99
00702274	Jazz Standards for Easy Guitar	$19.99
00702162	Jumbo Easy Guitar Songbook	$24.99
00232285	La La Land	$16.99
00702258	Legends of Rock	$14.99
00702189	MTV's 100 Greatest Pop Songs	$34.99
00702272	1950s Rock	$16.99
00702271	1960s Rock	$16.99
00702270	1970s Rock	$19.99
00702269	1980s Rock	$15.99
00702268	1990s Rock	$19.99
00369043	Rock Songs for Kids	$14.99

00109725	Once	$14.99
00702187	Selections from O Brother Where Art Thou?	$19.99
00702178	100 Songs for Kids	$14.99
00702515	Pirates of the Caribbean	$17.99
00702125	Praise and Worship for Guitar	$14.99
00287930	Songs from *A Star Is Born, The Greatest Showman, La La Land,* and More Movie Musicals	$16.99
00702285	Southern Rock Hits	$12.99
00156420	Star Wars Music	$16.99
00121535	30 Easy Celtic Guitar Solos	$16.99
00702156	3-Chord Rock	$12.99
00244654	Top Hits of 2017	$14.99
00283786	Top Hits of 2018	$14.99
00702294	Top Worship Hits	$17.99
00702255	VH1's 100 Greatest Hard Rock Songs	$34.99
00702175	VH1's 100 Greatest Songs of Rock and Roll	$29.99
00702253	Wicked	$12.99

ARTIST COLLECTIONS

00702267	AC/DC for Easy Guitar	$16.99
00702598	Adele for Easy Guitar	$15.99
00156221	Adele – 25	$16.99
00702040	Best of the Allman Brothers	$16.99
00702865	J.S. Bach for Easy Guitar	$15.99
00702169	Best of The Beach Boys	$15.99
00702292	The Beatles — 1	$22.99
00125796	Best of Chuck Berry	$15.99
00702201	The Essential Black Sabbath	$15.99
00702250	blink-182 — Greatest Hits	$17.99
02501615	Zac Brown Band — The Foundation	$17.99
02501621	Zac Brown Band — You Get What You Give	$16.99
00702043	Best of Johnny Cash	$17.99
00702090	Eric Clapton's Best	$16.99
00702086	Eric Clapton — from the Album Unplugged	$17.99
00702202	The Essential Eric Clapton	$17.99
00702053	Best of Patsy Cline	$15.99
00222697	Very Best of Coldplay – 2nd Edition	$16.99
00702229	The Very Best of Creedence Clearwater Revival	$16.99
00702145	Best of Jim Croce	$16.99
00702278	Crosby, Stills & Nash	$12.99
14042809	Bob Dylan	$15.99
00702276	Fleetwood Mac — Easy Guitar Collection	$17.99
00139462	The Very Best of Grateful Dead	$16.99
00702136	Best of Merle Haggard	$16.99
00702227	Jimi Hendrix — Smash Hits	$19.99
00702288	Best of Hillsong United	$12.99
00702236	Best of Antonio Carlos Jobim	$15.99
00702245	Elton John — Greatest Hits 1970–2002	$19.99

00129855	Jack Johnson	$16.99
00702204	Robert Johnson	$14.99
00702234	Selections from Toby Keith — 35 Biggest Hits	$12.95
00702003	Kiss	$16.99
00702216	Lynyrd Skynyrd	$16.99
00702182	The Essential Bob Marley	$16.99
00146081	Maroon 5	$14.99
00121925	Bruno Mars – Unorthodox Jukebox	$12.99
00702248	Paul McCartney — All the Best	$14.99
00125484	The Best of MercyMe	$12.99
00702209	Steve Miller Band — Young Hearts (Greatest Hits)	$12.95
00124167	Jason Mraz	$15.99
00702096	Best of Nirvana	$16.99
00702211	The Offspring — Greatest Hits	$17.99
00138026	One Direction	$17.99
00702030	Best of Roy Orbison	$17.99
00702144	Best of Ozzy Osbourne	$14.99
00702279	Tom Petty	$17.99
00102911	Pink Floyd	$17.99
00702139	Elvis Country Favorites	$19.99
00702293	The Very Best of Prince	$19.99
00699415	Best of Queen for Guitar	$16.99
00109279	Best of R.E.M.	$14.99
00702208	Red Hot Chili Peppers — Greatest Hits	$16.99
00198960	The Rolling Stones	$17.99
00174793	The Very Best of Santana	$16.99
00702196	Best of Bob Seger	$16.99
00146046	Ed Sheeran	$15.99
00702252	Frank Sinatra — Nothing But the Best	$12.99
00702010	Best of Rod Stewart	$17.99
00702049	Best of George Strait	$17.99

00702259	Taylor Swift for Easy Guitar	$15.99
00359800	Taylor Swift – Easy Guitar Anthology	$24.99
00702260	Taylor Swift — Fearless	$14.99
00139727	Taylor Swift — 1989	$17.99
00115960	Taylor Swift — Red	$16.99
00253667	Taylor Swift — Reputation	$17.99
00702290	Taylor Swift — Speak Now	$16.99
00232849	Chris Tomlin Collection – 2nd Edition	$14.99
00702226	Chris Tomlin — See the Morning	$12.95
00148643	Train	$14.99
00702427	U2 — 18 Singles	$19.99
00702108	Best of Stevie Ray Vaughan	$17.99
00279005	The Who	$14.99
00702123	Best of Hank Williams	$15.99
00194548	Best of John Williams	$14.99
00702228	Neil Young — Greatest Hits	$17.99
00119133	Neil Young — Harvest	$14.99

Prices, contents and availability subject to change without notice.

Visit Hal Leonard online at **halleonard.com**

1221
306

easy GUITAR play along

Audio Access Included

INCLUDES TAB

The *Easy Guitar Play Along*® series features streamlined transcriptions of your favorite songs. Just follow the tab, listen to the audio to hear how the guitar should sound, and then play along using the backing tracks. Playback tools are provided for slowing down the tempo without changing pitch and looping challenging parts. The melody and lyrics are included in the book so that you can sing or simply follow along.

HAL•LEONARD®
www.halleonard.com

Prices, contents, and availability subject to change without notice.

HAL•LEONARD GUITAR PLAY-ALONG

Complete song lists available online.

This series will help you play your favorite songs quickly and easily. Just follow the tab and listen to the audio to the hear how the guitar should sound, and then play along using the separate backing tracks. Audio files also include software to slow down the tempo without changing pitch. The melody and lyrics are included in the book so that you can sing or simply follow along.

INCLUDES TAB

VOL. 1 – ROCK	00699570	$16.99
VOL. 2 – ACOUSTIC	00699569	$16.99
VOL. 3 – HARD ROCK	00699573	$17.99
VOL. 4 – POP/ROCK	00699571	$16.99
VOL. 5 – THREE CHORD SONGS	00300985	$16.99
VOL. 6 – '90S ROCK	00298615	$16.99
VOL. 7 – BLUES	00699575	$17.99
VOL. 8 – ROCK	00699585	$16.99
VOL. 9 – EASY ACOUSTIC SONGS	00151708	$16.99
VOL. 10 – ACOUSTIC	00699586	$16.95
VOL. 11 – EARLY ROCK	00699579	$15.99
VOL. 12 – ROCK POP	00291724	$16.99
VOL. 14 – BLUES ROCK	00699582	$16.99
VOL. 15 – R&B	00699583	$17.99
VOL. 16 – JAZZ	00699584	$15.95
VOL. 17 – COUNTRY	00699588	$16.99
VOL. 18 – ACOUSTIC ROCK	00699577	$15.95
VOL. 20 – ROCKABILLY	00699580	$16.99
VOL. 21 – SANTANA	00174525	$17.99
VOL. 22 – CHRISTMAS	00699600	$15.99
VOL. 23 – SURF	00699635	$16.99
VOL. 24 – ERIC CLAPTON	00699649	$17.99
VOL. 25 – THE BEATLES	00198265	$17.99
VOL. 26 – ELVIS PRESLEY	00699643	$16.99
VOL. 27 – DAVID LEE ROTH	00699645	$16.95
VOL. 28 – GREG KOCH	00699646	$17.99
VOL. 29 – BOB SEGER	00699647	$16.99
VOL. 30 – KISS	00699644	$16.99
VOL. 32 – THE OFFSPRING	00699653	$14.95
VOL. 33 – ACOUSTIC CLASSICS	00699656	$17.99
VOL. 34 – CLASSIC ROCK	00699658	$17.99
VOL. 35 – HAIR METAL	00699660	$17.99
VOL. 36 – SOUTHERN ROCK	00699661	$19.99
VOL. 37 – ACOUSTIC UNPLUGGED	00699662	$22.99
VOL. 38 – BLUES	00699663	$17.99
VOL. 39 – '80s METAL	00699664	$16.99
VOL. 40 – INCUBUS	00699668	$17.95
VOL. 41 – ERIC CLAPTON	00699669	$17.99
VOL. 42 – COVER BAND HITS	00211597	$16.99
VOL. 43 – LYNYRD SKYNYRD	00699681	$19.99
VOL. 44 – JAZZ GREATS	00699689	$16.99
VOL. 45 – TV THEMES	00699718	$14.95
VOL. 46 – MAINSTREAM ROCK	00699722	$16.95
VOL. 47 – JIMI HENDRIX SMASH HITS	00699723	$19.99
VOL. 48 – AEROSMITH CLASSICS	00699724	$17.99
VOL. 49 – STEVIE RAY VAUGHAN	00699725	$17.99
VOL. 50 – VAN HALEN: 1978-1984	00110269	$19.99
VOL. 51 – ALTERNATIVE '90s	00699727	$14.99
VOL. 52 – FUNK	00699728	$15.99
VOL. 53 – DISCO	00699729	$14.99
VOL. 54 – HEAVY METAL	00699730	$16.99
VOL. 55 – POP METAL	00699731	$14.99
VOL. 56 – FOO FIGHTERS	00699749	$17.99
VOL. 57 – GUNS 'N' ROSES	00159922	$17.99
VOL. 58 – BLINK 182	00699772	$14.95
VOL. 59 – CHET ATKINS	00702347	$16.99
VOL. 60 – 3 DOORS DOWN	00699774	$14.95
VOL. 62 – CHRISTMAS CAROLS	00699798	$12.95
VOL. 63 – CREEDENCE CLEARWATER REVIVAL	00699802	$16.99
VOL. 64 – ULTIMATE OZZY OSBOURNE	00699803	$17.99
VOL. 66 – THE ROLLING STONES	00699807	$17.99
VOL. 67 – BLACK SABBATH	00699808	$16.99
VOL. 68 – PINK FLOYD – DARK SIDE OF THE MOON	00699809	$16.99
VOL. 71 – CHRISTIAN ROCK	00699824	$14.95

VOL. 72 – ACOUSTIC '90s	00699827	$14.95
VOL. 73 – BLUESY ROCK	00699829	$16.99
VOL. 74 – SIMPLE STRUMMING SONGS	00151706	$19.99
VOL. 75 – TOM PETTY	00699882	$17.99
VOL. 76 – COUNTRY HITS	00699884	$16.99
VOL. 77 – BLUEGRASS	00699910	$15.99
VOL. 78 – NIRVANA	00700132	$16.99
VOL. 79 – NEIL YOUNG	00700133	$24.99
VOL. 80 – ACOUSTIC ANTHOLOGY	00700175	$19.95
VOL. 81 – ROCK ANTHOLOGY	00700176	$22.99
VOL. 82 – EASY ROCK SONGS	00700177	$17.99
VOL. 84 – STEELY DAN	00700200	$19.99
VOL. 85 – THE POLICE	00700269	$16.99
VOL. 86 – BOSTON	00700465	$16.99
VOL. 87 – ACOUSTIC WOMEN	00700763	$14.99
VOL. 88 – GRUNGE	00700467	$16.99
VOL. 89 – REGGAE	00700468	$15.99
VOL. 90 – CLASSICAL POP	00700469	$14.99
VOL. 91 – BLUES INSTRUMENTALS	00700505	$17.99
VOL. 92 – EARLY ROCK INSTRUMENTALS	00700506	$15.99
VOL. 93 – ROCK INSTRUMENTALS	00700507	$16.99
VOL. 94 – SLOW BLUES	00700508	$16.99
VOL. 95 – BLUES CLASSICS	00700509	$15.99
VOL. 96 – BEST COUNTRY HITS	00211615	$16.99
VOL. 97 – CHRISTMAS CLASSICS	00236542	$14.99
VOL. 98 – ROCK BAND	00700704	$14.95
VOL. 99 – ZZ TOP	00700762	$16.99
VOL. 100 – B.B. KING	00700466	$16.99
VOL. 101 – SONGS FOR BEGINNERS	00701917	$14.99
VOL. 102 – CLASSIC PUNK	00700769	$14.99
VOL. 103 – SWITCHFOOT	00700773	$16.99
VOL. 104 – DUANE ALLMAN	00700846	$17.99
VOL. 105 – LATIN	00700939	$16.99
VOL. 106 – WEEZER	00700958	$14.99
VOL. 107 – CREAM	00701069	$16.99
VOL. 108 – THE WHO	00701053	$16.99
VOL. 109 – STEVE MILLER	00701054	$19.99
VOL. 110 – SLIDE GUITAR HITS	00701055	$16.99
VOL. 111 – JOHN MELLENCAMP	00701056	$14.99
VOL. 112 – QUEEN	00701052	$16.99
VOL. 113 – JIM CROCE	00701058	$17.99
VOL. 114 – BON JOVI	00701060	$16.99
VOL. 115 – JOHNNY CASH	00701070	$16.99
VOL. 116 – THE VENTURES	00701124	$16.99
VOL. 117 – BRAD PAISLEY	00701224	$16.99
VOL. 118 – ERIC JOHNSON	00701353	$16.99
VOL. 119 – AC/DC CLASSICS	00701356	$17.99
VOL. 120 – PROGRESSIVE ROCK	00701457	$14.99
VOL. 121 – U2	00701508	$16.99
VOL. 122 – CROSBY, STILLS & NASH	00701610	$16.99
VOL. 123 – LENNON & McCARTNEY ACOUSTIC	00701614	$16.99
VOL. 124 – SMOOTH JAZZ	00200664	$16.99
VOL. 125 – JEFF BECK	00701687	$17.99
VOL. 126 – BOB MARLEY	00701701	$16.99
VOL. 127 – 1970s ROCK	00701739	$16.99
VOL. 128 – 1960s ROCK	00701740	$14.99
VOL. 129 – MEGADETH	00701741	$17.99
VOL. 130 – IRON MAIDEN	00701742	$17.99
VOL. 131 – 1990s ROCK	00701743	$14.99
VOL. 132 – COUNTRY ROCK	00701757	$15.99
VOL. 133 – TAYLOR SWIFT	00701894	$16.99
VOL. 134 – AVENGED SEVENFOLD	00701906	$16.99
VOL. 135 – MINOR BLUES	00151350	$17.99
VOL. 136 – GUITAR THEMES	00701922	$16.99
VOL. 137 – IRISH TUNES	00701966	$15.99
VOL. 138 – BLUEGRASS CLASSICS	00701967	$17.99

VOL. 139 – GARY MOORE	00702370	$16.99
VOL. 140 – MORE STEVIE RAY VAUGHAN	00702396	$17.99
VOL. 141 – ACOUSTIC HITS	00702401	$16.99
VOL. 142 – GEORGE HARRISON	00237697	$17.99
VOL. 143 – SLASH	00702425	$19.99
VOL. 144 – DJANGO REINHARDT	00702531	$16.99
VOL. 145 – DEF LEPPARD	00702532	$17.99
VOL. 146 – ROBERT JOHNSON	00702533	$16.99
VOL. 147 – SIMON & GARFUNKEL	14041591	$16.99
VOL. 148 – BOB DYLAN	14041592	$16.99
VOL. 149 – AC/DC HITS	14041593	$17.99
VOL. 150 – ZAKK WYLDE	02501717	$16.99
VOL. 151 – J.S. BACH	02501730	$16.99
VOL. 152 – JOE BONAMASSA	02501751	$19.99
VOL. 153 – RED HOT CHILI PEPPERS	00702990	$19.99
VOL. 154 – GLEE	00703018	$16.99
VOL. 155 – ERIC CLAPTON UNPLUGGED	00703085	$16.99
VOL. 156 – SLAYER	00703770	$19.99
VOL. 157 – FLEETWOOD MAC	00101382	$17.99
VOL. 159 – WES MONTGOMERY	00102593	$19.99
VOL. 160 – T-BONE WALKER	00102641	$17.99
VOL. 161 – THE EAGLES ACOUSTIC	00102659	$17.99
VOL. 162 – THE EAGLES HITS	00102667	$17.99
VOL. 163 – PANTERA	00103036	$17.99
VOL. 164 – VAN HALEN: 1986-1995	00110270	$17.99
VOL. 165 – GREEN DAY	00210343	$17.99
VOL. 166 – MODERN BLUES	00700764	$16.99
VOL. 167 – DREAM THEATER	00111938	$24.99
VOL. 168 – KISS	00113421	$17.99
VOL. 169 – TAYLOR SWIFT	00115982	$16.99
VOL. 170 – THREE DAYS GRACE	00117337	$16.99
VOL. 171 – JAMES BROWN	00117420	$16.99
VOL. 172 – THE DOOBIE BROTHERS	00119670	$16.99
VOL. 173 – TRANS-SIBERIAN ORCHESTRA	00119907	$19.99
VOL. 174 – SCORPIONS	00122119	$16.99
VOL. 175 – MICHAEL SCHENKER	00122127	$17.99
VOL. 176 – BLUES BREAKERS WITH JOHN MAYALL & ERIC CLAPTON	00122132	$19.99
VOL. 177 – ALBERT KING	00123271	$16.99
VOL. 178 – JASON MRAZ	00124165	$17.99
VOL. 179 – RAMONES	00127073	$16.99
VOL. 180 – BRUNO MARS	00129706	$16.99
VOL. 181 – JACK JOHNSON	00129854	$16.99
VOL. 182 – SOUNDGARDEN	00138161	$17.99
VOL. 183 – BUDDY GUY	00138240	$17.99
VOL. 184 – KENNY WAYNE SHEPHERD	00138258	$17.99
VOL. 185 – JOE SATRIANI	00139457	$17.99
VOL. 186 – GRATEFUL DEAD	00139459	$17.99
VOL. 187 – JOHN DENVER	00140839	$17.99
VOL. 188 – MÖTLEY CRÜE	00141145	$17.99
VOL. 189 – JOHN MAYER	00144350	$17.99
VOL. 190 – DEEP PURPLE	00146152	$17.99
VOL. 191 – PINK FLOYD CLASSICS	00146164	$17.99
VOL. 192 – JUDAS PRIEST	00151352	$17.99
VOL. 193 – STEVE VAI	00156028	$19.99
VOL. 194 – PEARL JAM	00157925	$17.99
VOL. 195 – METALLICA: 1983-1988	00234291	$19.99
VOL. 196 – METALLICA: 1991-2016	00234292	$19.99

Prices, contents, and availability subject to change without notice.

Get Better at Guitar

...with these Great Guitar Instruction Books from Hal Leonard!

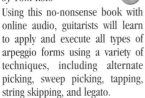

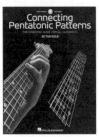

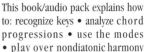